# STOP

## BEFORE YOU HAVE SURGERY READ THIS!!

by

Donald Donovan King

DORRANCE
PUBLISHING CO
EST. 1920
PITTSBURGH, PENNSYLVANIA 15238

Dorrance Publishing Co
585 Alpha Drive
Suite 103
Pittsburgh, PA 15238
Visit our website at *www.dorrancebookstore.com*

ISBN: 978-1-4809-9696-0
eISBN: 978-1-4809-9899-5

*I wrote this book despite suffering massive amount of brain damage from the stroke during the so-called routine neck surgery on March 10, 2015.*

# INTRODUCTION

M Y NAME IS DONALD KING. I am sharing my true story to the world, about a doctor and his assistant, who is a tumor specialist who misled me to do a very dangerous same day routine neck surgery, which almost cost me my life. I went to him for a consultation about a tumor that was growing in my neck. I thought it was cancerous but after he sent me to get it tested for cancer, I went back to him in a few weeks for the results. He told me that the tumor was benign. I asked him if he could shrink it because it was not bothering me or hurting me in anyway, shape, or form. My neck was just swollen where the tumor was located. The doctor told me although the tumor was not cancerous right now, if he shrunk it, it could still turn into cancer. And he said he was advising me just as he would a family member. He recommended he should just cut the tumor out and get rid of it. I got nervous when he told me that! Because I know that is too much trust to put in any human being to cut me open, no matter how much medical training they get. He told me not to worry about anything because removing tissue is very easy to do. He told me it is not like doing bone surgery, which is extremely painful. I asked him if I do the surgery, how many hours would it take? He said three hours, and I might spend the night in the hospital because it is a simple routine surgery. I asked how long would I be out of work? And he told me two weeks. But I told him I was still nervous; he told me not to worry because he has done thousands of tumor removals. And there was not one bad outcome. He convinced me very well to have the surgery. I told him I would come back in a few weeks to do the paper work because I was waiting for insurance.

I went home and did a Google search on the doctor and his assistant. And I did not find anything negative. In fact, US News and World Report said he is one of America's top doctors in his field. He works in several states because of his specialty. And his assistant is also a great doctor who assists eleven other doctors in several states as well. So that gave me some peace of mind. And I went back to his office a few months later to sign the paper work to do the surgery, and his assistant gave me the paper work to read. I read it and asked her about all the risk that was mentioned in the paper work, and I let her know about my concerns. She told me not to worry, and the paper work was just formality because I was not doing open heart surgery or brain surgery. And to prove her point, I would have a successful surgery. She gave me an appointment to come back one week later after surgery to see how it was healing. I did the surgery as they recommended, and the outcome was totally devastating for me and my family! I suffered a massive stroke during surgery and almost lost my life because a three-hour surgery became a fourteen-hour nightmare. The doctor and his assistant both lied to me just to get me into surgery to make the money. I know they kept putting me under anesthesia the entire time because when they were waking me up, I could hear everyone crying and freaking out! Only the right side of my body woke up. I was paralyzed on my left side. There was nothing routine about a fourteen-hour surgery. When they initially told me, it would last three hours. A blood clot was lodged deep in my brain. They ruined my life because I was unable to return to a normal life. This left me unable to care for myself and my family. Millions of families face serious health challenges every day. And if they can't get professional, honest opinions from their doctor to their health-related questions, how can they make good decisions for themselves or their family? The public is in bad shape because the government or the center for disease control or the health system is not going to protect us from these dishonest doctors. People need to protect their own interest. I think it is a good idea when you go for a consultation, make sure you are recording the conversation with the doctor on your cell phone. Therefore, you will have proof you can take in a court of law should something go wrong during your surgery because when I tried to sue the doctor, the lawyer told me that it was my word against his. When you go to sign the consent form for surgery, make sure you read every word from top to bottom. Make sure your family reads it as well because the form protects the doctors and the hospital, one hundred percent. You, the patient, have no protection. There should be no statute of limitation on medical negligence because when you try to get your medical records, they give you the run around and run out the clock on you. The law needs to change to remove the two years statute of limitations, so that the risk of surgery can be shared equally by doctors, hospitals, and the patient. The way it is right now, doctors have no incentives to be extremely careful because they know they will not be held accountable if something goes wrong. Just remember that stroke is the number one cause of disability in the world. How can anyone forget the sight of those disabled people in the nursing home in Houston, TX during Hurricane Harvey sitting in their wheelchairs helplessly as the flood waters rise around them. Because of their disabilities, they were not able to protect themselves. One could only imagine what they were feeling during that time!

# ACKNOWLEDGEMENTS

FIRST, I WOULD LIKE TO GIVE THANKS AND PRAISES TO GOD ALMIGHTY, our true and living savior, for sparing my life and pulling me back from death's door. Without his grace and mercy, I would not be here today to share my painful story with the world. I feel as though I was given a second chance at life. It made me cherish every moment and live life to its fullest.

Secondly, I would like to say much love and respect to my lovely wife, Josephine Craft-King, for being there for me when I hit rock bottom. She has been my tower of strength in which I could always rely. She has been with me throughout my perilous journey from day one until now. She has seen me make small but steady progress over the years. She literally saved my life with the help of God. And I can't thank her enough.

I want to also thank my sister-in-law Aletha Craft, who has been there from day one until now and always has my back.

I want to also thank Steven Walker, my dear friend who I affectionately call my brother from another mother. We have been friends for almost 40 years.

I want to also thank my dear friend and radio DJ, Selecta Jerry for always being there for me and my family. I also want to take this opportunity to thank his beautiful wife, Sister Beth O'Brien for the healing stone she gave me when they visited me in the hospital.

I would like to thank the many therapist, nurses, and caregivers at Marlton Rehabilitation Hospital for helping me with my rehab.

I would like to also thank Jamaican Dave Russell the promoter of the annual Reggae in the Park Festival at the Mann Music Center in Philadelphia for being a loyal family friend for over 20 years.

Donald Donovan King

I also would like to thank the entire WKDU 91.7 FM Reggae crew in Philadelphia, Pa. for the annual Reggae marathon that falls on my birthday almost every year.

Finally, I want to thank my fellow stroke survivors, warriors, and Facebook friends in my stroke support groups, where I can always go to get encouragement when I am feeling down and out. I LOVE YOU VERY MUCH, MY STROKE WARRIORS!

I did not know that I had the ability to write a book but I know that when someone survives a traumatic event in their life, like I did, it is much easier to tell my story.

My name is Donald King, and I am writing this book about my experience I had after I did a so-called same day routine neck surgery at a local hospital in Camden, New Jersey on March 10th, 2015 by a tumor specialist and his assistants.

I met this doctor two years earlier on October 6th, 2013 when I saw him in his Camden New Jersey office for my initial visit. I was referred by my local hospital for further evaluation after they found a tumor in my neck during a cat scan. He was very nice during my visit with him. He greeted me like he had known me for about 20 years. He looked at my neck and told me to make an appointment with the receptionist to come back to see him at his Voorhees, New Jersey outpatient office after this first visit. I told him I was waiting to get approved for health insurance because I didn't have any at the time.

It took me another six months to get approved for insurance. The insurance was approved on July 14th, 2014. I called the receptionist and made the appointment right away to see him at his Voorhees, New Jersey outpatient office.

This time when I went to visit him, he introduced me to his assistant and told me that she is one of the tumor specialist that works with him because he is the head doctor in charge of the ear, nose, and throat department. He also told me that on some occasions, she would be the doctor to see me when I visit because he also practices in other states because of his specialty. He gave me a prescription to get some testing done which included a MRI, a 24-hour urine analysis, blood work, and a dye test to make sure that the tumor was not cancerous.

All the tests took several weeks to get done because each test had to be done separately, and I had to take time off from work every time I had to do a test. Before I went back to him to get my test results, I did a Google search to check out both doctors and their credentials, and I did not find anything negative about any of the them; in fact, US News and World report said the doctor is one of America's top doctor in his field and his assistant is also a great doctor who works alongside 11 other doctors in other states. That gave me some peace of mind that I was seeing qualified doctors.

I went back a few weeks later to get my test results at his office, and he showed me a picture of a 3D carotid tumor rotating on his computer screen. He told me this is the tumor growing in my neck, and that is why my neck is swollen. He also said that those tumors grow about one centimeter a year, and he is going to discuss it at the next tumor board meeting. I asked him very clearly if it was cancerous, and he said it was benign, and I asked him if he could shrink it because it was not hurting me or giving me any problems. Surgery was the very last thing I was thinking about. He told me that if he shrunk it, it could still turn into cancer.

He said to me, "I am advising you like I would my own family, it is best for you to cut it out and get rid of it." He minimized the surgery to me by telling me that he has done thousands of these surgeries before, and removing tissue is much easier than removing bones which is extremely painful.

I was very afraid because the tumor was growing in my neck, and I feared it growing into my windpipe and cutting off my air supply. I asked the doctor how long would I be out of work if I did the surgery. He said the surgery would last three hours and that I might stay overnight in the

Donald King          My Stepson Timothy Craft

My ex-coworker and best friend
for almost 40 years Mr. Stephen Walker.

hospital because it is a same day routine surgery, but I was still nervous and anxious because that is a lot of trust to put in another human being to cut me open.

So, he convinced me, and I took his advice because he is a specialist in that field. Another reason why I decided to do the surgery is that one of my co-workers at the time had a cancerous spot on his face, and he refused to have surgery to have it removed. The cancer almost ate up half of his face. That is how quickly the cancer spread. When he finally went and had the surgery, he lost his sight in his right eye and was unable to return to work. For many months, I did his shift before they found another driver to fill his place.

If it was heart surgery or brain surgery, there is no way I would do any surgery like that, unless I had a major accident and ended up in the hospital against my will.

The way that the doctor explained the procedure to me, I was assured that I was in good hands. I explained to him that I could not be out of work for a long period of time. I am a taxi driver, and I have a lot of customers that ride with me every day for many years, and they depend on me, so I had to protect my customer base and support my family. If I do not work, I do not get paid.

I made an appointment with the front desk to come back and do the paper work for the surgery. I had to get approval from the insurance company 30 days in advance before any surgery is permitted.

On November 1st, 2014, I went back to his office to sign the paper work for surgery and this time, his assistant was in the office. She gave me the paper work to sign. I read it and asked her about all the risks. She told me not to worry because my surgery is very easy and routine. She explained to me that it is not open-heart surgery or brain surgery, which is very risky. And to prove her point, she gave me an appointment to come in the office seven days after the surgery to remove stitches and to see how the wound is healing.

I asked her if she was going to use the cyber knife to do the surgery, and she said the tumor was too big to use the cyber knife, so she would be using an old fashioned surgical stainless-steel knife to make a half inch incision under my neck to remove the tumor.

I spent an hour or more talking to her about other surgeries like mine that she had done before. She told me that she had removed larger tumors than mine in the past from other patients, and their outcome was fine.

She also minimized the surgery in my mind just because they wanted the money. If they had shrunk the tumor, they would have gotten less money. So, they went ahead and risked my life by doing a very dangerous surgery just to get the money that left me paralyzed.

Now that I look back at what happened, I was facing a very difficult situation with the tumor growing in my neck; they gave me November 18th, 2014 to do the surgery. So, when I received the welcome letter from the hospital, it was addressed to me but when I opened it, it said Dear Mr. Marshall. At this point I got nervous because my name is Donald King and not Mr. Marshall. I've heard of too many bad stories of patients getting operated on by mistake. I called the hospital and pointed the discrepancy out to them, and they apologized to me and sent me the right welcome letter with my name on it.

At this point, the holidays were right around the corner, which was my busiest time of the year to make money for my very successful taxi business.

I was not willing to do surgery during the holiday season and risk being away from my family and customers. So, I went back on January 15th, 2015 to sign the paper work again to do the surgery on February 18th, 2015 but I got sick with the flu. I was not able to go and get the surgery done. I went back two weeks later and signed the paper work for the last time to do the surgery on March 10th, 2015.

They sent me to get pre-admission testing done a week before surgery. I went to the hospital on March 3rd, 2015 and got the test done. On March 10th, 2015, I went in for surgery. I went to the waiting lounge accompanied by my wife and my sister-in-law because I was given clear instructions before-hand to bring someone with me to the hospital because I would not be able to drive after the surgery or take public transportation home until the anesthesia wears off.

I got there at exactly 9:30 AM. The doctor met us in the waiting area and told me in the presence of my wife and my sister-in-law that everything would be just fine, and we must not worry about anything. He hung out with us for about an hour before the nurse came to get me at about 11:00 AM. Then I was taken in to be prepped for surgery. That was the last thing that I remembered. My wife told me that I was in surgery from 11:00 AM Tuesday morning until 1:00 AM Wednesday morning. The surgery lasted for 14 long hours.

The next thing that I remembered, they were waking me up, screaming, crying, and yelling "Oh my God, I'm freaking out. Something went wrong." Just the right side of my body woke up. My wife told me that the doctor called the waiting room and told her that there was little movement on my left-side after surgery, and I was being checked out by the neurologist. The neurologist ruled out that I hadn't had a stroke. About an hour later, the surgeon went down to the waiting room and had a meeting with my wife, my sister-in-law, and my daughter and explained that I was in ICU for further observation.

*appointment after Surgery*

**◉ Cooper**
University Physicians
**Cooper Medical School of Rowan University**

**University Otolaryngology Associates**

### Yekaterina Koshkareva, MD

| | | |
|---|---|---|
| Three Cooper Plaza | 6200 Main Street | Washington Township |
| Suite 411 | Voorhees, NJ 08043 | 2 Plaza Drive |
| Camden, NJ 08103 | Phone: 856.325.6516 | Sewell, NJ 08080 |
| Phone: 856.342.3275 | | Phone: 856.270.4150 |
| Fax: 856.361.1939 | | |

CooperHealth.org          New Patient Appointments: 856.342.3113

Front of Appointment card to see Dr. after Surgery

M *Donald King*
has an appointment on

❑ Monday    ☑ Tuesday    ❑ Wednesday
❑ Thursday    ❑ Friday    ❑ Saturday

Date *3/17/15*          Time *8:45AM*

Location *Voorhees Office*

If unable to keep appointment, kindly give 24 hours notice.

Donald Donovan King

Donald King

# Cooper
University Health Care

Division of Otolaryngology – Head and Neck Surgery

Three Cooper Plaza
Suite 404
Camden, NJ 08103

ph: 856 342 3275
fax 856 361 1939

CooperHealth.org

**Nadir Ahmad, MD, FACS**
Division Head
Director, Head & Neck Cancer Program
Associate Professor

**Nathan A. Deckard, MD**
Director, Rhinology, ENT Allergy
& Skull Base Surgery

**Dean A. Drezner, MD, FACS**

**Molly Hammond, APN**

**Jagdeep S. Hundal, MD**

**Yekaterina Koshkareva, MD**

**Thomas C. Spalla, MD**
Director, ENT Facial Plastic Surgery

**Karl V. Whitley, MD**

**Audiology Department**

**Meghan L. Pavlick, AuD**
Senior Audiologist

**John M. Davis, AuD**
Clinical Audiologist

**Rachel Olanoff, MSPA**
Clinical Audiologist

**Cooper Medical School**
of Rowan University

### AM ADMISSIONS/OUT PATIENT INSTRUCTIONS
### PLEASE READ THE ENTIRE PACKET

Your surgery is scheduled on ___3/10/15___ with

*Assisting*
**Dr. Nadir Ahmad**    **Dr. Nathan Deckard**    **Dr. Jagdeep Hundal**
**Dr. Thomas C. Spalla**  (**Dr. Yekaterina Koshkareva**)

**Cooper University Hospital** ✓
Same Day Surgery Department will call to confirm the time of surgery and special instructions the day before between the hours of 4:30PM and 8:00PM

A parent or legal guardian (only if the patient is a minor) must accompany the patient to and from the hospital. They must remain in the hospital while the patient is in the operating room.
Following anesthesia, you must not, under any circumstances operate a motor vehicle or use any sort of machinery until the next day. The accompanying adult should make sure the patient is taken back safely to their home by personal auto. Public transportation is not acceptable.
If general anesthesia or sedation is used ( ✓ YES  NO____ ).
It will be necessary for preliminary blood work and/or studies to be performed at least 2-3weeks before your surgery. If ordered by your surgeon, a pre-admission order slip will be enclosed in your packet. You can make an appointment at Three Cooper Plaza or any other Cooper Out Patient Pre-Surgery Testing sites.
The number is (856) 342-3149.

Your stomach should be empty and no food or drinks should be taken after midnight the night before your surgery.
Do not take aspirin or aspirin-containing products at least 1 week prior to surgery.

If you need additional information or need to cancel or postpone your surgery, please call the office at 856 342-2051 or 856 342-3275 prompt 2.

Please call if your health insurance and/or your phone number have change.

Thank you for choosing the Cooper Health System. *during Surgery.*
*Donald had a stroke during Surgery.*
*Donald was left paralyzed on his left side.*
*He is disabled.    JCK*

8

 Cooper
University Hospital

**HealthCare Access**

One Cooper Plaza
108 Pavilion
Camden, NJ 08103

ph. 856.342.3118
fax 856.968.8461

CooperHealth.org

February 27, 2015

Mr. Donald King
162 Millbridge Road
Clementon, NJ 08021

Dear Mr. King,

Welcome and thank you for choosing Cooper University Hospital. On behalf of our entire staff, we wish you a comfortable and speedy recovery. Your care and treatment is of utmost importance to our staff. The minute you step through our doors, you become our number one priority. At Cooper, every employee is committed to providing a safe, high-quality healthcare environment that is personalized for each of our patients. This means our excellent care is given in combination with kindness and concern for your personal situation. It takes many professionals in a variety of different jobs working in harmony to meet this challenge.

We look forward to your arrival on **March 10, 2015** for your scheduled surgery. For your convenience, you will be called by our hospital staff with the time of your admission. To ensure effective and efficient processing, please be sure your lab work has been completed as requested by your physician. If your insurance requires a pre-certification for your scheduled surgery, it is the responsibility of your surgeon to obtain the pre-certification from your insurance company and notify Cooper University Hospital at least 48 hours prior to your surgery. If you have any questions regarding your insurance, please contact an Insurance Specialists at (856) 356-4850 Monday through Friday 7:30AM to 4:30PM. Please find a Patient Information Guide enclosed. We ask that you take a few minutes to familiarize yourself with all that Cooper has to offer. The information will help you get to know the services we provide and more than likely answer any questions you may have in advance.

We recommend that you try to limit the number of personal belongings you bring on the day of your admission. If this is not possible your nurse will be happy to have your valuables placed in our hospital safe. Personal care items such as dentures, eye glasses and hearing aids can be easily stored in the bedside table.

We are pleased to have the opportunity to care for you. Allow yourself to take comfort in knowing that you have made the right choice. At Cooper, you will receive both personal and serious care with attentive and compassionate hospital staff.

Best regards,
Linda A. Brand, Director
Patient Services Center

 **Cooper Medical School**
of Rowan University

I am in ICU, and my wife and daughter came back to see me, and they were crying, and I remember my daughter saying, "Daddy, I love you, and please don't die."

They left the hospital, and my wife said, "I'll be back later." I called my wife at 7:00 am to let her know that I suffered a massive stroke during surgery which resulted from a blood clot that was lodged deep in my brain. The CAT scan revealed the blood clot earlier before they took me to ICU. I was paralyzed on my left side, and I could not move. They put tubes through my nose into my stomach for tube feeding me. I was so weak, I could not sit up in the bed without assistance from the nurses and even then, I was falling to the left-side like a log. I had double vision; I could barely see anything or hear anything. I could not swallow anything at all because my swallowing was so weak that they had to take me to the basement of the hospital to do a video swallow test that showed that I was aspirating, which means every time I swallow liquids, some would get in my airways and end up in my lungs which would give me pneumonia. I was not allowed to drink any liquids unless they put thickener in it.

I was also put on all puree food because I could not eat any solid foods whatsoever. As a result, I was very hungry, thirsty, and dehydrated. When they put the thickener in the liquids, it tasted very nasty like I was drinking starch. I asked the nurse how do I get over this swallowing problem? Before she could answer me, another doctor came in and was trying to convince me to surgically implant a feeding tube in my stomach. I asked him if this would give me another stroke? He told me it was not without risk.

I said to him, "I had a stroke less than 12 hours ago, and you want to cut me again?" He did not answer me and I told him to go to hell. When he left, I asked the nurse again, what are my options? She told me to either put in the feeding tube or go to speech therapy because my speech was also paralyzed.

I was very depressed, and I could not make sense out of what was going on with my situation. Before I did the surgery, I was very fit and strong. I worked every day, seven days a week, and I've never been sick or on any type of medication ever. I used to go to the gym three days a week for the past ten years. I bench pressed 200 lbs. always at the gym. I've never had high blood pressure or any other ailments and here I am, laying in the hospital bed unable to help myself or my family. At this point, I felt like a real loser because my whole life style has changed within in the past 24 hours.

I am a very responsible person as a self-employed individual. Before I even scheduled the surgery, I went ahead and paid up my life insurance policy, paid off my credit cards, paid off my car loan, and paid up my rent three months in advance. I also saved an additional $3,000.00 cash just in case something went wrong. I paid my rent for March the same day I had the surgery, just to buy myself some time, although the doctor told me that I would be back to work in two weeks.

Later that day, the doctor who did the surgery came to visit me in ICU and told me that the tumor was bigger than he thought, and that is why the surgery took so long. He apologized to me and told me that he put me on blood thinner to rush blood to my brain to break up the blood clot. When he told me that, I was feeling very hopeful that everything might be fine. So, I asked what if I am unable to return to work for a while; at this point, that was my main concern.

He told me not to worry because the hospital had social workers that would come to my room and help me with all my concerns.

After spending three days in the ICU, I was put into a regular room at the hospital with the feeding tube in my nose and a catheter in me. During all this time, I was very traumatized. I couldn't do anything on my own. I had lost my independence and my dignity.

I spent another three weeks in the hospital, unable to do anything for myself. Just laying there, looking up at the ceiling. The nurses had to bathe me right there in the bed and feed me with a spoon when it was time for me to eat or take my medication. I was so upset and hurt because at age 53, I knew it would be very hard to bounce back from a stroke like this because it was induced from the surgery. I did not get this stroke naturally. They were operating on me too long. Even a horse would have a stroke if you operate on him for 14 long hours, much less a human being.

After spending three weeks in the hospital, I was then transferred by ambulance to Marlton Rehabilitation Hospital in Marlton, New Jersey. I was still bed ridden for another month and a half. My left foot was swollen, and my left arm was paralyzed. The therapists rehabilitated me enough until I could sit in an alarmed wheelchair and walk just a little bit. My physical therapist, Anna, was very patient and kind when she was teaching me to walk. My occupational therapist, Brianna, was very patient and kind to me as well when she was teaching me to say my alphabet's and different brain games. My speech/pathologist therapist, Kelly, was very professional and kind when she was teaching me to learn how to talk again, monitoring my swallowing ability and taught me different facial exercises to massage my mouth back in place because it was very twisted to the left from the stroke. They all help rehabilitate me for a month and a half until I was wheelchair ready to go home.

My dear wife was the biggest victim. She went through the living hell with what happened to me. She was up and down the road, back and forth to the hospital, trying to work and not to mention all the mountains of paper work she had to fill out for me to get my social security disability benefits, and years of back and forth to different doctor's appointments all over the state of New Jersey.

I was blessed to have a strong person to help care for me and nurture me back to be strong enough to continue my quest for recovery. I was not able to return to my upstairs apartment that I had lived in for the past 20 years because I was unable to climb the steps. My wife had to get a first-floor apartment before I was released from the rehab.

I did not see this happening to me. I lost my business that I worked very hard to build over the past decade, driving taxi in Lindenwold NJ, and I was about to branch out and start another one on Fort Bragg NC. This is the largest special forces base in the country. I made good money driving those guys around. All that planning came crashing down on March 10th, 2015 after my devastating surgery, just because I trusted the wrong doctors.

If a patient can't trust a doctor, who can you trust? This doctor lied to me, plain and simple, by telling me that the surgery was routine. There is absolutely nothing routine about a 14-hour surgery when he initially told me it would take three hours, that is why I asked him how long it would

Marlton Rehabilitation Hospital where they bring me back as best as they can

last because if he had told me it would last six hours, I would not have done the surgery. I would have found another way. I think that the law should require that whatever advice, suggestions, instructions, and every word that a doctor speaks to a patient in his official capacity should be recorded for patient protection. When I tried to sue the doctor for paralyzing me, I told the lawyer that the doctor told me that the surgery would take three hours, but it took 14 hours. The lawyer told me that it is my words against the doctor. I could not believe what I was hearing.

A medical research study that was released on May 3rd, 2016 shows that medical errors are the third leading cause of deaths in the United States of America. By studying medical deaths rate data over an eight-year period, the patient safety experts have realized that more than 250,000 deaths per year are due to medical error in the U.S., their figure surpasses the U.S. Center for Disease Control Preventions third leading cause of deaths, respiratory disease, which kills almost 150,000 per year. The research team states that the CDC way of collecting national health statistics did not classify medical errors separately on death certificates.

My physical therapist Anna,

that taught me to walk again

Marlton Reh Therapist,

Brianna my occupational therapist (R)

and Kelly my speech Therapist (L)

The researchers are advocating for updated criteria for classifying deaths on death certificates. In their study, the researchers examined four-separate studies that analyzed medical rate data from 2000-2008, then using hospital admission rates from 2013, they saw that based on a total of 35,416,020 hospitalizations, 251,454 deaths stemmed from a medical error, which the researchers say now translate to 9.5 percent of all deaths each year in the US. According to the CDC in 2013, 611,105 people died of heart disease. 584,881 died of cancer, and 149,205 died of chronic respiratory disease, the top three causes of death in the U.S. The newly calculated figures puts this cause of death behind cancer but ahead of respiratory disease. Top causes of death, as reported by the CDC, informed the country's research funding and public health priorities; researchers say right now cancer and heart disease gets maximum attention, but medical errors are ignored by the CDC.

More research needs to be done to prevent medical errors, which is a huge problem in this country. How many more people are going to die before they take this problem seriously?

My occupational therapist Kristin who is working with
me to get my hand working again.

I have researched everywhere to see if I could find any research or
any data about patients who have become disabled because of medical
error and I could not find anything whatsoever. I think that it is safe to
say that no such data or research exists now. But I am willing to be cor-
rected if I missed any research, study, or data. Because I am left disabled
after a medical error and put on social security disability, I am sure there
are thousands of other patients left in similar situations, which put unnecessary burden on the Social Security Disability program, hospitals, and
doctors who are found to be negligent in their duties and violate the public trust should be forced to reimburse the Social Security Disability program for monies that have been paid to injured patients, so that the
program can remain solvent for future generations and for the purpose
for which it was intended.

We need a very strong patient bill of rights in this country. The wild-
wild west medical mentality in this country needs to stop. There need to

be tough federal laws against predatory doctors, medical officials, and medical institutions.

These people take an oath to cherish, protect, and save lives. The patient's well-being and health must be and should be the number one priority of any medical professionals in this country; it should be the platinum standard by which all medical institutions are judged because there is nothing more sacred and precious than life itself.

Patient protection in America is very weak, and I believe that every surgery in the United States should be videotaped, no matter how small the procedure, is from beginning to end. The video will not lie, and it will show the most detailed part of any operation at any given time.

When the doctor told me that the surgery would take three hours during my consultation with him, if all of that was written down and three hours into the surgery an alarm would have gone off, that might have helped me to avoid the stroke and save me another 11 hours of butchering. I cannot believe that someone who has been through years of training would put another human being through so much suffering and pain.

After the surgery, I was living my worst nightmare. My wife did extensive research on line to find an advocacy group, and all she found was this one lady living in Texas and her 22-year-old daughter had died during surgery. She was unable to get any justice or compensation for her loss, so she formed her own advocacy group, and she encouraged my wife to start her own advocacy group in New Jersey, but all we wanted was to make some sense out of what happened to me.

Two years after the horrible outcome of my surgery, I did a lot of soul searching to see where did I go wrong. I went back and read the doctor's profiles again on the internet, and I was shocked to see that this doctor only has 17 years of experience and his assistant has only 11 years' experience. She graduated from medical school in Philadelphia in 2006, and she was the one who did the actual cutting of my neck during the surgery. And the doctor with the 17 years of experience was the one in charge of that entire Ear, Nose, and Throat surgery department. He was her boss.

It is an outrage that these large hospitals and medical industrial complex have these young doctors doing surgeries on patients. It takes nine years to train a physician and 12 years to train a good surgeon and another three or four years for their residency training at numerous hospitals and clinics. So, where is the experience here?

Now, I remember the first time that I met this doctor for consultation, I was very surprised to see how young the doctor was. Not one strand of gray hair was on his head. I asked him how old he was, and he said 42. I said you are very young, Doc. That was a huge red flag to me. I know that if you do not have any gray hair in your head, then your experience is not very deep because he told me that he was the head doctor in charge of the Ear, Nose, and Throat department. I gave him the benefit of the doubt, and after reading his profile on line which it stated by US News and World Report that he was one of the top ten doctors in America in his field in 2011-2012, which was very impressive at such a young age. His profile is still on the internet for anyone to read right now. That is why I went along and did the surgery because I thought he was good.

Great doctors have 20, 30, or even 40 years of experience in their field of expertise, so they can always give patients good solid advise.

The surgeon that opened my neck on March 10th, 2015 had only nine years of experience at that time if she graduated from medical school in Philadelphia in 2006, when I back tracked the years to the date when she did my surgery, that is the only experience she had. With that limited amount of experience, the hospital has her operating on patients. Her profile is still on the internet as well for everyone to see.

It is virtually impossible to hold a doctor accountable for malpractice or negligence because they hide behind the consent form that a patient signs, giving them and the hospital permission to do surgery. The form tells the patient that if anything goes wrong during the surgery, they are not responsible, although the doctor is doing the surgery in the facility of the hospital. That is the most ridiculous nonsense I've ever heard of. The system has allowed them to reign terror on innocent patients, for example, look at the opioid crisis raging across America right now. 64,000 patients died in 2017 because doctors over-prescribed highly addictive powerful pain killers. For someone to recover from addiction, you must give it all you got, that is why the moment the doctor prescribes me any type of medication, I trashed it immediately. This is a dire warning to anyone who plans to do any type of surgery or operation. The most important thing that you must do is to read the consent form that you are about to sign to give the doctor and the hospital permission to do your surgery. Take as much time as needed to read the consent form repeatedly. Do not rush to read it or let anyone rush you to read it. The next thing you must do is check to see how many years of experience the doctor has in his or her field of expertise.

Great doctors get their training from all over the world. They do not graduate from just one medical school. Patients need to put in time and effort to do proper research on doctors. Make sure you see gray hair on his or her head, which is usually a sign of vast knowledge and experience. Be very careful of young doctors. Most of the time they are a few years out of medical school and owe huge student loans, and they will give you very bad advice just to make money. Many times people go to the doctor on their lunch break from their work and rush and sign papers they did not read. That is a very bad idea. If you are planning to go to the doctor, make sure you take a day off from your job, so you can focus like a laser beam on what the doctor is telling you because sometimes what they are telling you is 100% different from what you are about to sign. All they care about is the almighty dollar, not you.

The doctor told me that the appointment card that he gave me to come back to him seven days after my surgery super cedes any paper work that I signed to do my surgery because it is directly from the department that he oversees. I remember when I went to sign the consent form to do my surgery and the doctor brought me the form, she was trying to distract me by being overly nice by asking me all types of unrelated questions about various things. Then she quickly said to me, I have some papers for you to sign. She did not ask me to read these papers and sign them. I was the one that asked her to let me read what I was signing, and she said sure. I should not have to ask to read the papers giving them permission to do my surgery because my life is the one at risk.

When I read the paper and saw all the risks that I was facing, I was scared to death. Especially the part that says they are not responsible if anything goes wrong during the surgery. The doctor assured me that it was just formality, and I should not worry since my surgery was a same day routine neck surgery which would last no more than three hours, and I might spend over night in the hospital after surgery. They lied to me. If I can prevent one person from enduring the horror that I've been through by not experiencing this endless nightmare, then my effort is worth it.

These mega hospitals are so large, they are like small cities that employs thousands of people. How does a patient know for sure that when you see a doctor in one of these hospitals they are a real doctor? Patients do not have access to a doctor's school records, grades, or any other personal information about them. We must rely on what the hospital tells us or what we google on the internet, which can be bogus information.

Who is really watching to make sure that no one with bad intentions falls through the cracks?

In 2012, an 18-year-old Florida teenager who pretended to be a doctor's assistant and treated patients in a hospital emergency room was jailed for a year. He was found guilty of working in a regional medical center emergency room in Florida for almost a month, changing bandages, IV drips, and conducting physical examinations on patients. He also performed CPR on a patient who suffered a drug overdose. The county courthouse judge heard that the teenager had access to confidential medical records and had worn scrubs and a stethoscope, used a pager, and bought a lab coat. He was convicted of two counts of practicing medicine without a license and two counts of impersonating a physician assistant in August 2011 when he was 17. He was arrested in 2011 and released on bail, but in January 2012, he was back in police custody, this time for impersonating a police officer. He told the investigating officer he had originally gone to the hospital to get a badge for his job as a clerk at a doctor's office across the street, but he was entered as a physician assistant in the computer by mistake. The only reason he got caught, he was asking to be let into highly secured areas.

One would think this was an isolated incident, but a few years later, another Florida teenager managed to fool an entire medical center into thinking he was a doctor for an entire month before he was found out. The teenager wore a white coat that said anesthesiologist on the back as he walked through the corridors of the medical center in Palm Beach, which was widely reported at the time. He presented himself to patients by saying, "welcome to our practice" and introduced himself as Dr. Robinson. The teenager managed to fool the security guards who work at the facility. He was discovered after being caught in an examination room with a patient while wearing a mask and a stethoscope. The security told police that the boy was known at the medical center as a doctor and had been seen going and coming out from secured areas according to a police incident report. Police and the hospital agreed not to prosecute the boy after his mother told them he was under doctor's care and had refuse to take his medication for an unspecified illness.

Does anyone know how many more imposters are still out there posing as doctors? If no one knows the answer to this question, then we are all in serious trouble.

There are very few professions on this planet with the sacred responsibility to preserve and protect human life, like a pilot and a doctor. When you get on a plane, the pilot has full control over your life, 100%. It is up to the pilot's ability and competence whether you make it to your destination or not.

In 2017, there were at least three incidents where pilots were arrested by officers at the airport just before boarding the aircraft because they were about to fly the plane intoxicated, which was filled with passengers. The same cannot be said about a doctor who is about to perform surgery on a patient. I have never heard of a doctor getting caught being intoxicated or high on drugs before doing surgeries. There is no one watching them, so patients have no way of knowing if they are intoxicated or high on drugs.

When a patient is being operated on, the doctor controls your life 100% because you are laying there while they are operating on you. It totally depends on their ability and competence whether you live or die.

I have been getting Botox injections in my left arm since 2015 until now, which is a very expensive drug that cost thousands of dollars for each injection. I get the injections every three month, which must be administered by a doctor, and my left arm is still not working. I have been very frustrated by this whole situation, doing years and years of therapy, and the left arm is stubborn as a mule. I hope it doesn't take decades before my left arm is healed. I will by a very old man by then.

Medical malpractice or negligent should include the over prescribing of medications that a person can get addicted to. The doctors should be held accountable by affected patients and their families. We need congress to pass a bill that removes statute of limitation from medical malpractice cases, and you will see less deaths and suffering.

I remember when I was in the hospital recovering from my surgery, I was unable to get any rest whatsoever because people would be coming in and out of the room all day and all night, drawing blood, taking my temperature, or giving medications. I was unable to tell the difference between the nurses and the cleaning crew because they all wore scrubs.

One day, I was laying in the bed, and I asked the nurse who was assigned to me if I could please get some water to drink and she said ok, I'll be right back, but she did not return. I was laying there helpless, just looking at her walking back and forth, pacing the hallway, looking in at me each time she passed my room. There was absolutely nothing I could do but lay there and look. That's what being disabled mean.

I think that it would be a great idea for the American Disability Association to join with Aflac and establish a disability bank for helping anyone who suddenly become disable either by an accident or if they wake up one morning and find themselves disabled, everyone is one accident away from finding out that this can happen to them, especially people that do very dangerous jobs. Employees and self-employed individuals could save a small portion, tax-free dollars towards this program.

When I became disabled at the age of 53, I was so traumatized from what happened to me, and I was even more traumatized by worrying if I was going to get approved for my Social Security Disability benefits because most people who apply have been denied the first time. In my stroke support group, there were many stroke survivors that have tried several times before getting approved years later; during that time, while they are waiting to be approved, they lost everything. I met a young man that had a stroke when he was 46-years-old and two years later, he is still waiting to hear from them, and he is in the process of losing his house. He is living with his mother and her husband.

If there was a private disability fund to fall back on, we could avoid unnecessary suffering. Many small business owners like taxi drivers, beauticians, and barbers collect cash for their services, but many of them do not pay into social security, so if something happened to them, they have nothing on the books to collect if they become disabled or when they reach old age. That is why I always stress to my friends the importance of working on the books because if I did not do that years ago, I would have found myself in a world of trouble and if there was a disability bank, I still would have had money saved in my account. This would have given me an additional income every month.

Last year in 2017, 10,000 disabled individuals died while waiting for their disability claims to be processed. If you are waiting for the government to protect you, good luck. Over 37 million Americans are disabled, about 12% of the total population. More than 50% of those disabled Americans are in their working years from 18-64. Most working Americans underestimate their risk of disability. Disability causes severe financial hardship. 90% of wage earners rate their ability to earn an income as valuable or very valuable in helping them achieve long-term financial security. Wage earners know that their ability to earn an income is even more valuable than retirement savings, medical insurance, personal possessions, other forms of savings, or their homes. Medical problems contributed to 62% of all personal bankruptcy filed in the US in 2007. An estimate of over 500,000. This is a 50% increase over results from a similar 2001 study. Medical problems contributed to half of all home foreclosures in 2006. Few American workers are financially prepared if something goes wrong. 68% of adult Americans have no savings for an emergency. 65% of working Americans say they could not cover basic living expenses even for a year if their employment income was lost, 38% could not pay their bills for three months. Nearly nine in ten works, (86%) surveyed believe that people should plan in case an income-limiting disability should occur. Most American workers income is not protected. About 100 million workers are without private disability income insurance. 69% of workers in the private sector have no private long-term disability insurance. Do you think social security or workers compensation will cover it? You better do your home-work. That is why I mentioned earlier that we need a disability bank ur-gently in the USA with branches in all 50 states and territories that can process disability claims within a 24-hour period to give disabled people peace of mind.

The only security blanket a disabled person has is how much money they have access to at any given time to keep a roof over their head and to pay for living expenses. The ultimate mission of a disability bank is to get disabled people back on their feet.

I did not have the privilege of such an institution to fall back on after the doctor left me as a disabled invalid. I was paralyzed with fear thinking about what would happen if the Social Security Administration denied my disability claim because they had denied me SSI two times in June 2015. I was terrified to death. But the good Lord smiled down at me, and they ap-proved my Social Security Disability claim five months later when I was flat broke.

I cannot stress enough how grateful I was, and I still am for that lifeline. That doctor really put me in a major crisis and a serious bind. Doctors mis-conduct has reached an alarming level, and I haven't heard one word from any medical association denouncing their behavior.

In the final analysis, these medical associations and the federal gov-ernment silence is deafening

Where is the outrage from the public?

When I was growing up as a child, I was taught by my mother that a man is supposed to take care of his family, he is the one who should bring home the bacon, and I have abided by that principle all my life until that came to an end on March 10th, 2015. It literally breaks my heart to see how hard my wife must work at her job and come home and take care of all my needs without help from anyone because every family must shoulder their own burden.

I know, for sure, if this doctor never left me paralyzed after that botched surgery I would have a booming business by now with many em-ployees. I am blessed to live in one of the most unique areas of the US, which is known as the Delaware Valley, which includes the state of

Delaware, New Jersey, and Philadelphia. This area is about an hour and a half from New York City, 40 minutes from Atlantic City, 20 minutes from Wilmington Delaware, two hours from Baltimore, Maryland, and two and a half hours from Washington, DC. And that is why I went into the taxi business because the earning potential is unlimited. When I use to take a passenger to New York John F. Kennedy airport for example, I can go home for the rest of the day after doing such a trip.

My business was 20 minutes away from Philadelphia, although it was based in Lindenwold, Southern, New Jersey. The whole area is still the Philadelphia Tri-State area, where we get our news, sports, and weather from.

Philadelphia is one of America's oldest iconic historic cities with every major sports teams and world class facilities, including major Ivy League Universities, many large hospitals and one of the largest airports in the North East United States, where I transported many passengers over the years to catch their flights.

There is always some type of function going on in Philly where I use to take customers like the annual New Year's Eve Ball, The Flower Show, The Auto Show, various music festivals of all kinds, and other large scale events throughout the city seven days a week, all year round, and that's what keeps the taxi drivers busy going back and forth across the Ben Franklin Bridge from South Jersey in and out of Philly.

I got really upset when the Pope visited Philadelphia in the fall of 2015 and all I was able to do was watch it on TV, The Democratic National Convention was held there in the summer of 2016, the NFL Draft was held there in 2017, but the most painful event for me, was when the Philadelphia Eagles Football team won their first super bowl championship in history for the city and millions of fans like myself and from around the world.

All those massive events that took place in Philly while being out of work due to my disability, brought millions of people to the city and billions of dollars to the city in transportation, hospitality, sightseeing, and trips to the Jersey shore. My ex co-workers told me that business has never been better during the years I have been out of work.

It makes me sad about my situation being that I was not able to work during this time, but because I am not a lazy person I am now a writer. For anyone reading this, who is going through a challenging or a rough time, please do not give up. Try doing some writing yourself to tell your story because every heart knows its own bitterness and it is good therapy.

When I do recover no one will give me a job because I will be too old to go into the work force. I must depend on my own initiative and life experience to survive. Because of this doctor's negligence, I was deprived of my true potential in life, and the pursuit of freedom and happiness. I am pleased to be able to tell my story, because no one should endure the extreme pain and suffering that I am enduring until this day.

Please be aware of bad decisions when it comes to having surgery which can cause an extreme life changing situation for you and your family. Man do not plan to fail in life, man fail to plan.

I contacted a personal injury lawyer, and he told me to come into his office to do some paperwork. He told me he would review the paperwork and call me, and we would go from there. After waiting to hear from him for about four weeks, I called him to see what was going on, and he asked me what was my case about again. I told him it was about having a massive stroke during surgery that left me paralyzed. I told him that the doctor had lied to me because he said that the surgery would last three hours and it lasted for 14 hours, which lead to me having the stroke. The lawyer told me that he is not sure if there is any penalty for a doctor lying to a patient, so he referred me to a medical malpractice lawyer in Cherry Hill, New Jersey.

The lawyer called me and asked me a lot of question pertaining to the surgery. He told me he would be mailing a package of paper work to read, sign, and return to his office as soon as possible. The paperwork came in three days. I read it, signed it, and returned it to him. I called to make sure that he got the paperwork. He said he had received it, and he would call me if he needed more information from me. Two months later, I called him to inquire about the case. He told me he was waiting for my medical records. I waited for another two months before I called him again, and he told me he was still waiting on my medical records. So, I waited another three months and called him again, and he sounded very upset as if I was bothering him. I waited another two months before I called him again, and he told me he had sent off my medical records to be studied by experts. Three weeks later, I got a letter in the mail from his office informing me that he was unable to do the case, and I should seek other counsel. I contacted another lawyer who took all my information over the phone, and he also sent me a package of information to read, sign, and return to his office, which I did. I called the office a few days later to make sure that they had received the paperwork. The secretary told me they received the paperwork, and I should call back within a month. I called back, and she told me that they could not take the case. My wife did some research online and found a lawyer in Philadelphia that had represented a person in a similar case just like mine. I called them, and they took all my information over the phone, and they mailed me a package of paperwork to be signed and returned to their office. I called the office to see if they had gotten the paperwork, and the secretary told me that the lawyer would call me as soon as he reviews the case. I waited a month and did not hear from him, so I called to find out what was going on, and the lawyer told me he was waiting for my medical records, so call I him back in a month. When I called him back, he told me that the hospital was giving him the run-around handing over my medical records and I should call him back in the next 30 days. I gave him some extra time, so I called him back in 45 days, and he said he was still waiting for my medical records, and he would call my wife once the records came in.

The lawyer called my wife three months later and told her that he had received all my medical records and he had reviewed them, and he would not be able to take my case to trial because he would have to put out about $200,000.00 dollars and if he lost the case, he would be out of all that money. So, he advised me to seek counsel elsewhere, and he reminded me that I had one year left before the statute of limitation run out from this point on. He mailed me all my medical records on a compact disc. I contacted three more lawyers after that, but they all took so long to research my case that the statute of limitation ran out. All my legal options had run out. I found it to be very strange that not one of the five lawyers that I've contacted had ever asked me to come into their office to at least look at my physical condition. All the information they got from me was over the phone, although I have an after-surgery appointment card to see the doctor seven days after the surgery for them to see how the incision was healing. This is a written proof that I held onto in case something went wrong. I told the lawyers about this key piece of evidence that I had, but they were not interested. At this point, all my legal options had expired.

I called the State Attorney General Office, and they told me to call the State Medical Board, which I did, and all they did was give me the run around. So, I went to my congressman, Donald Norcross in Cherry Hill, New Jersey, and his secretary told me to call the state crime victim's unit. And when I called them, they told me that they only help violent crime victims. I even contacted my insurance company that paid for the surgery, and they told me that they could not provide me with any information. So, I called the hospital administrators office and explained to them what had happened to me, and they promised to call me back, and they never did.

I was really blessed to have survived a massive stroke like the one I had and live to tell about it. Any good doctor would go above and beyond their duty to do due diligence to make certain that none of their patients suffer a stroke under their care. A stroke is the ultimate destruction of the human body. A stroke can leave you blind, speechless, paralyzed, and even death. What upsets me the most is if I had died during surgery, they would have blamed me and told my family that they did not know that I was that sick. They would have covered their tracks very well.

I've heard of instances where they would go into a person's medical records and change it if an investigation was closing in on them. There should be no statute of limitation on medical malpractice.

My life has been changed permanently. I am suffering greatly, physically, emotionally, and mentally in every way possible. I lost my independence, my business, my way of life, and my ability to work and support my family. I have become totally helpless and useless to myself and my family. I can't tie my own shoe laces, put on my clothes or bathe myself. I have become totally dependent on other people to take care of me. This is a dreadful experience. I would never, ever want my worst enemies to experience anything like this. There are times that I wish I was dead and be out of my misery, so I won't have to endure such humiliation and pain.

I was raised by a single mom, and I've been working since I was 11-years-old and being independent was all I knew because in 1971, my mother went to the hospital to get a procedure done, and she did not come back home from the hospital, and at age 11, I became an orphan. After that, I've never trusted doctors or hospitals.

A family friend of ours, that we had not seen for over ten years, was hospitalized for kidney failure and when we went to the flea market to sell some peppers and compact discs, a lady came to the table to buy some peppers, and she was talking and I recognized the voice, and she asked my wife if her name was Lisa. My wife said yes, and she said I'm Gloria. And we were shocked because we didn't recognize her at all. She had picked up a serious infection in the hospital that had disfigured her facial appearance so bad, as if someone had thrown a bucket of acid in her face. We cried and hugged her and exchanged phone numbers. We called her the following weekend to check on her progress and to encourage her and give her moral support.

Before my surgery, that was the first time in my life that I've been hospitalized. While I was laying there in the hospital bed, I was thinking about the hundreds or thousands of patients who have died in this same bed. Hospitals are a breeding ground for infections, strokes, and death. A patient will check into the hospital, but it is not a sure thing that you will come out alive and well. They do not see you as a patient, they treat you like a customer. They try to keep you in the hospital if they can to charge you more for your stay. If you do not have someone advocating for you, you are in big trouble because they had me on a medication that had me coughing very hard. My wife had to tell the head nurse that the side effects of the medication is what was making me cough so badly, and she demanded that they take me off that medication, and I stopped coughing in less than 24 hours. My wife had to constantly complain to them about keeping my room clean, emptying my trash can and my urinal.

When I went home from the hospital, the insurance company gave me five weeks of in home therapy, which did not help me a whole lot, so I signed up to go to outpatient therapy rehabilitation at Marlton Rehabilitation hospital for another three months. During that time, I made very little progress, and they released me and wished me the best. My left arm was not working at all, and my walking was very, very weak. I was very lucky that my right side, which is my dominant side, was not affected by the stroke. So, I could function a little. The other problem that I had was brain damage from the blood clot that is lodged in my brain from the surgery. As a result, I became very forgetful, and I must constantly check behind myself, especially after using the bathroom and during a conversation.

After my rehabilitation ended, I signed up to get Botox injection therapy in my left arm every three months to see if I could get my arm to work again. It is now over two years since I've started getting the Botox injections in my left arm, and my arm is still not working. The stroke deformed my body to the point where I am bent out of shape, literally. My arm feels very heavy, like I am swinging a bag of rocks. My fingers are folded up so tight that I constantly use my right hand to do everything. I do electroshock therapy to see if that would help to re-educate the nerves and eventually open my fingers. That has not helped up to this point. So, I am now using a resting splint to see if that will work. It is now safe to say I am a disabled person.

This is my new reality that I must come to live with. All the precautions that I put in place to help me and my family out after the surgery was not nearly enough after I suffered the stroke. All the money that I saved up to pay bills and other living expenses were all gone after a few months, and my wife carried the load. Her income was all we had to live on until finally they approved my Social Security Disability benefits after five months. That was truly a blessing from God himself because a lot of people were telling me it could take up to six years to be approved. That was a huge relief and a life line for me and my family. Prayers do come true when you pray from the heart, I did not know that I would be so happy to receive that little check per month, that is what I was reduced to, after I was almost making that amount in one week from my job. It was a good thing that I had the wisdom and the foresight to pay into Social Security from the beginning as a self-employed person, or else my situation would have been very bad for my family and I.

The lesson here to anyone who is reading this and is self-employed, make sure you pay into Social Security and pay your taxes because if not, you can find yourself in a very bad situation that can bring a crisis to you and your family. I used to go to stroke support group meetings at Marlton Rehabilitation hospital once per month after my stroke, and I heard some real horrific stories of people losing homes, cars, and everything that they had worked for because they did not pay into Social Security. As a result, a lot of people end up in the poor house.

Those doctors stole my future away from me. I miss going to work every day, playing with my grandkids, cutting the lawn, taking trips with my family. I miss driving, planting my garden in the springtime, shoveling snow in the winter, going fishing, traveling, dancing, swimming, going to the gym, and hanging out with the guys. It is very hard to do these now because of my disability. All the things that I used to do by myself, I have pay someone else to do for me, which is very frustrating because most of the time, people can't be bothered. They promise to show up and they don't; for me to have one hand working is very dangerous. It is hard for me to defend myself if someone tried to attack me when I go for a short walk to exercise my legs. My neighbor was walking her pit bull dog at the same time I was going for my regular evening walk, and I came face-to-face with her and her dog. The dog rushed at me but luckily for me, she held on tightly to his leash, and he pulled her to the ground flat on her face. God was on my side that evening. If that pit bull had gotten to me, he could have done some serious bodily damage to me because he has bitten others in the complex including children. Before I go out in the evening, I scope out the area to make sure there is no danger lurking because there is also a flock of wild turkeys that lives in the forest behind my house that chase the neighborhood children from time to time.

I feel very vulnerable and insecure, so that is why I avoid crowded areas like malls, grocery stores, concerts, or anywhere there is a large gathering. So, my wife always takes me to the park or by the lake where I can walk without being disturbed by anyone. I get very sad, angry, and jealous when I see people in their 60's, 70's, 80's, and even in their 90's driving and going about their business without a care in the world and here I am, in my early 50's, and all I can do is sit, look, and wish. As a former cab driver, I was used to a type of freedom, I used to be all over the place. I could stop and eat wherever I wanted to, I could go to the park and drop back my seat and sleep on a beautiful day on my down time. I would stop by my house as often as I liked when I was working. I did not have to look over my shoulders, I was my own boss, and I used to make good money doing something that I liked. All my customers were very nice, we were like family. I have customers that rode with me from the time they were kids until they become adults.

Two of the wild turkeys that harasses me when I'm walking around the block

Gazebo where I rest
after a long walk

Blackwood Lakes where I go
to sit and listen to the waterfalls

Donald King taking a break from a long walk at K-9 memorial park

Veterans Memorial Park, where I go to walk to strengthen my legs

Donald King walking in Veteran's Park. Gloucester Township, New Jersey

Beautiful Blackwood Lakes

Watching the ducks swimming in Blackwood Lake on a quiet Sunday afternoon

My pet duck (Don dada)

My best friend Skip and I are the same age, and he is out having a great time, kite surfing, playing sports, and playing with his dogs. I was deprived of all of that because of my paralysis. One of the neurologist who saw me a week after the surgery told me that the doctor who did my surgery told her that my surgery was the most difficult surgery that he has ever done. That is why when half of my body woke up from the surgery, they were freaking out so bad. They realized that they almost killed me.

Immediately after the surgery, the doctor went to Dubai on vacation. He called me at the rehabilitation hospital from Dubai, and he apologized to me for what had happened. He told me that the tumor was wrapped around the main vein leading to my brain, and he said he had peeled it off, and he did not see any signs of physical damage at the time, he said if there is any damage, it must be on the inside of the vein. And I had mentioned this to all the lawyers that I had talked to. And none of them listened to me. That was so wrong. I walked to the hospital in perfect shape, and I left out of there in an ambulance to Marlton Rehabilitation where I spent all of Easter 2015 until they released me to my wife in a wheelchair on May 2$^{nd}$, 2015. Before they released me, she had to come in for training for three days to learn how to take care of me when I got home and set her up with caregivers support groups here in New Jersey because she was very traumatized as well.

Being a caregiver, she had to get familiar with setting up special equipment's for the bathroom, such as grab rails, shower bench, high toilet seat, helping me to take a shower, and making sure I did not fall. She still had to go to her job and carry my portion of the load. That was a huge life changing experience for her because she must do everything by herself now and taking care of me at the same time, while I sit in my wheelchair, just looking at her, waiting for my next meal, a shower, my medication, or for her to push me outside in my wheelchair to get some fresh air. I could see how stressful my situation made her, but I understand. It is a good thing that I did involve her in my cab business while I was working. She did not have a cab license to drive a cab but when I got extremely busy, I would call her and ask her to pick up a few customers for me in her personal vehicle and because of that, she had her own little customer base. She had one family that liked riding with her and no one else because she is a safe driver and has never had an accident in her life. While I was out with the stroke, they kept her very busy, so that helped us out a whole lot financially. They called her almost every day for a ride to take them to various places. At this point, they are more like family than customers, they have invited us to their company picnics, to church, to baby showers, end of year Christmas party, and other family functions.

The Herrara family my most valuable customer when I was driving taxi

I did physical exercises at home for the rest of 2015, all of 2016, and still, there is not a lot of progress, but I am not giving up. It is now 2017, and I am still working extremely hard to get better and to get my life back on track, but it is very hard. A lot of people have been encouraging me to stay strong, but they have no clue how I feel inside.

Stroke is very demoralizing. When I go out in public, walking with my cane and limping, people look at me funny. They have no mercy for disabled people. So that is why I stay home a lot to avoid crowded areas or anywhere there is a lot of people, especially at the mall where young people hang out. They are very inconsiderate. They will knock you down and run away and laugh about it because they think it's funny. I've seen it done plenty of times before this happened to me.

My shower bench

Exercise pedal used
to strenthen my legs

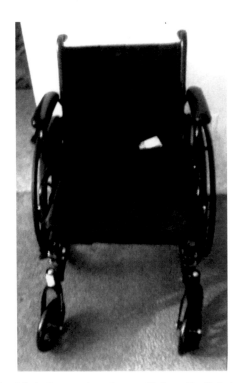

My wheelchair they sent me home with from the Rehab Center

I am grateful for the support cast that I have. If it had not been for that, I would have been dead a long time ago. They literally kept me alive. I cannot thank them enough. I also thank God for giving my family the strength to take care of me and not get sick themselves. My situation is long term care, and I need their help daily. Six months after I was released from the Rehabilitation Hospital, I was taking a shower on my own, and I fell in the bath tub and hit my left ribs on the edge of the tub. I thought I had broken my ribs because it hurt so bad. I could not get out of the tub. I was very lucky that my sister-in-law was home, and she helped my wife pull me out of the bath tub. I was blessed that I did not hit my head on the edge of the bath tub, that would have killed me because when someone is on blood thinner like I am, and if they fall and hit their head, they will die from bleeding in the brain. God was on my side that day, and I thank God that I did not break my ribs; by my left hand not working, I was unable to balance myself. If I am falling, I cannot grab onto anything to stop me from falling.

I am very happy that I treated my family well when I was on my feet because after the stroke, there was an out pouring of support from my friends, customers, and co-workers. I really appreciate all the love and support that I got from everyone wishing me a speedy recovery. My co-worker always stops by to check on me to see how I am doing and giving me words of encouragement to get better and hurry back to work. It makes me very sad to hear about the amount of money my co-workers are making driving the cabs as the economy improves.

When I started in the cab business 11 years ago, gas prices were almost $4.00 per gallon, and business was very slow because the economy was sluggish at the time. The moment that I had the stroke and could not work, gas prices became dirt cheap. The average gallon of gas came down to $1.60 per gallon and even cheaper in some places, and I miss all of that.

In my opinion, having a stroke is worse than death itself because when someone dies, you are not a burden to yourself or anyone else. Still, I am very happy to be alive, but I would not be here today without excellent care from my family and therapist that genuinely wanted to see me get better. Without proper care, I would not be here to tell my story. My

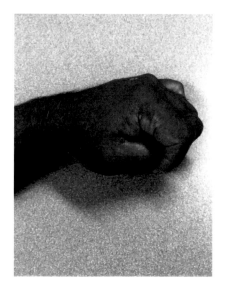

Swollen affected hand

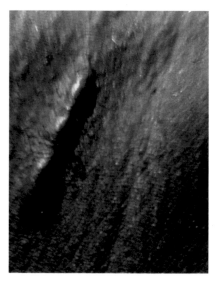

A close up of the nasty
scars left by the surgeon's knife

My new hand splint
without my hand in it.

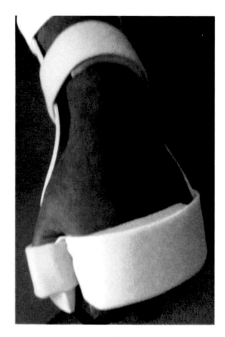

My hand in my new
hand splint

This is an old iron that I use
to do exercise with paralyzed hand.

Dycem sticky material that I use
when I eat my meal so that the plate
doesn't move around.

My arm getting electro-shock
therapy to wake up the nerves.

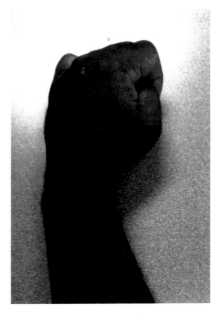

My paralyzed left hand

struggle has been unreal. I often ask God why this happened to me because I have always been a good person and treated others kindly and with respect.

I honestly thought I was doing the right thing by listening to the doctor. When I asked him earlier if he could shrink the tumor, I think if he had considered that, the outcome might have been much better or if he had given me a series of treatment over a period of time, then I think I may not have needed the surgery. I think he exercised very poor judgement. As the old saying goes, a good carpenter should measure twice and cut once. The lesson here for anyone reading this book is when it comes to doing any type of surgery, large or small, get at least several opinions, if you must. Because you are sadly mistaken if you think some of these crooked doctors have the patient's best interest at heart. Money is the only thing motivating some of these doctors. You are literally taking your own life in your hands when you go to these doctors.

This is the t-shirt I was selling online for fundraising purposes

How can anyone justify the amount of people who have died every year in the hospitals? I am hoping someone will do something about this waste of human capital, which is bad for the economy in general. The more than two years of income that I've lost is a huge blow to my family and my neighborhood. Although I am only able to use my right hand, I went online trying to sell stroke survivors t-shirts and sweatshirts, but that was unsuccessful because not everyone had a stroke, so I changed the writing to say I Am a Survivor, and I only sold nine shirts.

Times are very tough because I can't go out and work to take care of my family, and it makes me feel like I have no purpose in life. I feel so helpless, I can't find words to describe such feelings. I could have just kept quiet and said nothing but what they have put me and my family through has changed our lives forever, that's is why I'm writing this book to let the whole world know what they did to us and hope this will never happen to anyone else. Right now, I will not go back to any doctor, unless it is absolutely necessary. By no means am I telling anyone not to go to the doctor but from my personal experience, they always find something wrong with you, even if you are feeling perfectly fine. Thirteen years ago, my sister-in-law went to the doctor to get a checkup, and the doctor told her that he found a pulp near her heart, and she should go and have surgery to remove it because it could grow larger and cover her heart and eventually cause death. She ignored his advice until this day, and she has not had any problems whatsoever. We are the same age, and she is just as fit as can be. So, it is ok to ignore your doctor's advice from time to time.

The surgery that I had has weakened my body so much that I feel that 1 am not going to live that long. Once again, I am asking everyone to be very suspicious of every doctor. I am living proof that my doctor lied to me, and they will do the same to anyone. I took myself off the blood thinner that he had me on for the last two and a half years because it has terrible side effects like making me feel nauseas, bleeding for hours after shaving if I got a little nip from the razor, and unexplained bruises all over my body. My vision changes from time to time. Most of the medications that these doctors prescribe does more harm than good. Everyone should just listen to those drug commercials on TV and listen to all the side effects, and you

The company that I leased my vehicle from for the past decade

Lindenwold train station that I operated from for the past 10 years

Me and my ex-coworker Ed Lampe.

will see for yourself that the side effects outweigh the benefits. Everyone should be afraid of blood thinners because if you are on it and you become involved in an accident, you will bleed to death quickly. I am now taking 325 milligram coated aspirin twice per week, along with guinea hen weed tea, which is a natural blood thinner that has no side effects, and I feel 100% better. I can now shave my face as smooth as my hand middle. If I get a small cut, I will bleed for no longer than five minutes. One of my Facebook friends who knew of my problem introduced me to the guinea hen weed tea. I did some research on it myself and found out that the guinea hen weed plant is a perennial that is native to the Amazon Rainforest and other tropical areas of the Caribbean, South, and Central America; it is sometime called garlic weed as it can give off a strong garlic odor. Guinea hen weed uses have a long history of healing results and in more extreme cases, to induce an abortion. The herb can be used to make a soothing beverage. Guinea hen weed tea is becoming popular among cancer patients who have been told by their doctors there is nothing more that can be done for them. The tea is made with an extract taken from the stems and leaves of the plant. Those who plan to use the tea to treat medical conditions are warned that the tea alone is not a cure, it should be used with proper nutrition, rest, supplements, and acid detox. The tea should be taken on an empty stomach. The guinea hen weed plant has been known to have positive effects when used by cancer patients in addition to many other ailments, such as inflamed joints, rheumatism, weakened immune system, and arthritis. Studies have shown that use of the herb tea increases the body's natural ability to defend itself against diseases, so it naturally boosts the immune system. The stronger your immune system, the less risk of diseases or cancerous cells developing when the immune system is boosted. Extract from the herb have long been used to relieve pain caused by arthritis, inflammatory problems, and rheumatism. These pain-relieving properties have been proven in studies conducted in laboratories. There are many testimonies from all over the world because of taking guinea hen weed tea for cancer. It is recommended to use organically grown guinea hen weed in this form; it is free of pesticides. As a powder, you can add one tablespoon of guinea hen weed to a liter of water. The tea can be consumed half cup per day for relieving tumors, cancer, and leukemia. I am so sorry that I have never heard of guinea hen weed until recently or else I would have taken it sooner, although people all over the world have been using it for thousands of years.

When I called my local natural health food store and asked them if they carried guinea hen weed tea, the manager said he had never heard of guinea hen weed tea before, so I do wonder why all this information about such a powerful healing herb is not widely available to the public. My suspicion is that the less people know about natural alternatives to pharmaceuticals medications, they will spend more money buying drugs that is harmful to themselves without checking other options. Guinea hen weed is not for everyone, especially pregnant women or people who are taking blood thinners. My whole family is now drinking guinea hen tea, and they are using it for different symptoms. It can be purchased on eBay or on Amazon. For further information about this powerful herb, go to guineahenweed.com and learn more about it. You will be amazed.

The powerful Guinea Hen weed tea bags that cures
more than 70+ illnesses in the human body

I am also using Turmeric, which is the source of curcumin. The plant is very well known in India. The root is harvested, cleaned, dried, and crushed into a powder and used as a spice in curry powder to give it a beautiful yellow golden color and as a very powerful medicine. The curcumin extract from the turmeric has many health benefits. It stops pain, inflammation, and tumors. It fights cancer, burn fat accumulations, regulates blood sugar, stops depression, and slows Alzheimer disease. It is very rich in vitamin C that keep people from catching the flu or a cold, which is great for people with very weak immune system. Turmeric can be consumed in a hot glass of milk, in soups, in cooked foods. I use one table spoon of Turmeric with a pomegranate fruit (remove the skin from the pomegranate). Put the pomegranate in the blender with fresh broccoli and blend well to make a smoothie. Pour into a glass and drink with a straw, so it will not discolor my teeth. Then I refrigerate the rest. I drink it for nine months to prevent prostate cancer.

Fresh Tumeric.

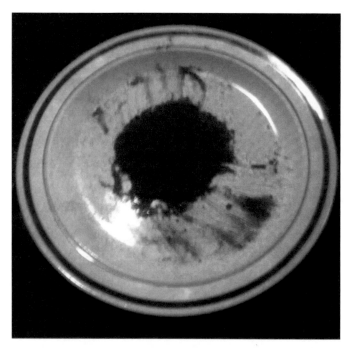

Turmeric powder that is good for inflammation and good blood circulation

Tumeric mixed in fresh milk.

These are some of the ways that I've gotten creative to help my healing process along with my music therapy. I am a huge reggae and smooth jazz fan. I listen to music at least eight hours a day and any chance I get. Music is a comforter for the heart, mind, and soul. It makes me forget about all my problems. It is my natural high. It takes me to places in my mind which I've never been before. I would like to thank my dear friend and reggae deejay Selector Jerry on Tunein.com for dedicating the four hour show to me on Saturday March 14th, 2015 while I was in the hospital after I had the stroke. I would like to also thank his wife Beth for coming to the hospital and the rehab hospital to visit me and giving me a beautiful healing stone.

I would recommend to anyone who is struggling, suffering, or trying to heal from sickness to develop their own music therapy regiment that is right for themselves. They should listen to the type of music that they enjoy and after a few months, they will see a big difference in their recovery. They can buy a portable bluetooth wireless music system and listen to music on it streaming right from your phone. They can take it to the park, to the beach, or to the family reunion. I love reggae music and smooth jazz so much. That helps me to keep going on from day to day. So, I take my music system with me where ever I can.

Hanging out with Jerry O'Brien host of Sounds of the Caribbean on Tunein.com.

My portable sound system that I use for music therapy

I also came across a cure for back pain, which is another big problem in America and all over the world. People are suffering so much from back pain and all you can see on TV are commercials advertising surgeries to relieve back pain. That type of pain is so excruciatingly dreadful that people would do anything or spend any amount of money to get some relief and because of that, many people get addicted to their pain medication and have serious constipation problems. I was prescribed pain killer medication for my back, but I did not like the side effects, so I asked the doctor to prescribe me a different medicine and that one was worst, and I stopped taking any type of pain medication.

One of my long-time customers and Facebook friend has been suffering with back pain for over 15 years. All the way back to her early 30's when I just met her as my customer. 1 remember her always crying about her back hurting her, and I took her to different doctors all over south Jersey. Sometimes they would give her pain medication that helped a little, but she said the medication kept her constipated for weeks. And sometimes they would give her the cortisone injection near her spine and that would ease the pain for a few days. But the pain would then return, which makes it difficult to function. She had to call out from her job a lot. Earlier this year in 2017, someone told her to try yoga. She did it for 12 weeks, and it worked for her perfectly. She is now 100% healed and has no more back pain. She jogs everyday now, which she was unable to do before. She's now able to go shopping at the grocery store and walk the entire store without riding the mobile carts that's reserved for the handicapped. When she told me that she was healed, I could not believe it. Four nights later after she told me that, I was watching the 11:00 o'clock news on my local ABC station and on the health check segment of the news, they reported they had found out that yoga is a cure for back pain. The segment was very brief. So, I went to do some further research on what they had just reported. I found a study in the Annals of Internal Medicine published June 2017 that found that yoga works as well as physical therapy for healing back pain. A randomized trial found that in both yoga and physical therapy, participants achieved reduced pain and disability, and about half reduced their drug use. People apparently liked yoga better. I would like to tell all my friends to try yoga for back pain. It is cost effective, it can be done at home or in a group. Just imagine the millions of people who might have done unnecessary surgeries that we may never know about that could have done yoga years ago.

The human body has a way of healing itself naturally over a period of time when you take good care of it and consume the right foods and lots of water. During this time of my healing process, I am making sure that I eat a lot of fruits and vegetables during breakfast, lunch, and dinner. I drink turmeric tea with fresh lemon in it every night before bed. It flushes my kidneys and keep my blood pressure normal. I drink guinea hen weed tea before breakfast every morning so that my body can properly absorb it. I do not smoke cigarettes or drink any type of alcohol. The only day of the week that I eat meat is for Sunday dinner with rice and beans. When I eat eggs, I only eat the egg whites and throw out the yolks because it will clog your heart. I walk every chance I get, and I go to the gym where I walk in the salt water pool to help improve my balance and strengthen my muscles because the human body was made to move and to keep proper blood circulation throughout my body.

I tried to keep an upbeat and positive attitude always because my emotional, mental, and spiritual state is just as important as my physical well-being. I go to church every chance that I get to worship and interact with my fellow church members. I also visit my stroke support group on Facebook daily to see and hear what is going on in the group. I find it to be very informative and helpful to everyone in the group who is trying to recover. We lift each other's spirits, and we call ourselves warriors because we are all fighting a very unusual battle that most people do not understand.

My wife is also recovering with me being my caregiver. She had to find a caregiver support group on Facebook as well so that she can see what other care givers are going through, so that she could get some feedback from other caregivers who are going through the same experience as she is going through. She still does a lot of paper work for me, although I had the stroke more than two years ago, she must prove that my brain injury from the stroke has not suddenly gotten better and that I deserve the little bit of Social Security Disability Benefits that I receive monthly.

After I had the stroke, I put on a whole lot of weight because I was sitting and eating and not doing any exercising. I am now eating smaller portion, drinking lots of water, and started exercising again. I drink my water at room temperature because ice cold water is not good for the human body, especially after eating a hot meal. Whenever the ice-cold water meets the hot food in the stomach, it hardens the food and forms one big blob in the stomach that takes a very long time to be digested and broken down by the body; as a result, that is what causes a lot of people to be obese. After a meal, it is best to drink a hot cup of tea, hot soup, or any other warm beverage so that the food can be digested properly and broken down in the body instead of it just sitting there in the stomach, which can make a person feel very sick. Ice cold water will give some people very bad headaches. People who suffers from migraine headaches should not drink ice cold water because it will make their headache worst.

Me and my church brother Rick who was in rehab with me in 2015

Aletha, Donald and Josephine after church

I do not use cold water at my house for any reason. All we drink is room temperature bottled water. We do not drink water from the tap because some of those water mains are well over a hundred years old, which makes them rusty on the inside and if you drink bad water like that, it will take a doctor a very long time to diagnose my problem. Drinking fountain drinks from restaurants is very dangerous. Just remember that if those restaurant workers forget to clean the fountain dispensers properly with bleach every night, germs will grow in it and can cause some deadly bacteria to get in your system. You can get sick to the point of where the bacteria can kill you. That is why I do not drink fountain drinks, and I limit my intake of sugary drinks, sodas, and ice tea, which can give you a kidney stone or other kidney infections. I drink at least four or five bottles of water every day to flush my kidneys. Green tea with lemon and honey is also good for you. Sleepy-time tea is also a good tea for people who are having a hard time falling asleep at night, especially true for people who are recovering from a stroke or other related illness. Sleepy-time relaxes you and help you to get a good night rest naturally without taking sleeping pills.

Stroke patients feels so tired every day, it makes them doze off a lot and at night, it is very difficult for them to sleep. It makes you lose your appetite because when you eat, the food keeps spilling out of your mouth on the affected side. You are always drooling at the mouth on the affected side of the mouth. I must always have a napkin in my hand to wipe my mouth constantly and when I go out with my wife to eat, she's always reminding me to wipe my mouth and the sad thing about it, I do not feel the food coming out of my mouth or when I am drooling because the left side of my mouth is still numb after all these years. Heavy saliva is always building up in my throat, I have coughing episodes and if I cough too hard, it gives me the hiccups badly. I'm always feeling like food is in my throat no matter how long ago I've eaten. Whenever I drink anything, I must drink it very slowly because I choke very easily.

I always feel like I am learning. My clothes never feel like they are straight on me. I cannot wear regular pants with a belt anymore. I can't wear any shirt that buttons or zip up the front. I can only wear sweat pants with an elastic waist band or shorts with an elastic waist band. I can only wear pull over shirts. In the winter time, I cannot put on my jacket or my coat. I stay inside most of the winter to avoid slips and falls when there is snow and ice storms. I must stay out of the cold weather because it affects my muscles so bad on the side where I had the stroke that my muscles retract so much that it feels like concrete and extremely painful. My eyes play tricks on me. There are times that I feel like I have grits in my eyes. Sometimes I will be looking at an object and it's like I'm not seeing it, although I am looking at it. I have bad headaches most of the time because of the blood clot that is lodged deep in my brain. I feel like I've had a concussion when I have the headache.

I am educating myself about what I consumed so that I can preserve my life, that I can live to an old, ripe age. Life is the greatest gift that has ever been given to mankind. I realize that when I was watching an episode of my favorite reality television show "The Deadliest Catch" on the Discovery channel when one of the crab fisherman was having a heart attack on the fishing boat in the middle of the Bering sea, and the captain of the boat called in the coast guard. I watched that brave coast guard helicopter pilot and his crew fly out to the fishing boat, risking their own lives to let down a rescue basket on the deck of the fishing boat in very rough 30-foot seas to extract the fisherman from the deck of the boat to take him to the hospital. It was amazing to see how the pilot let the basket down between all the equipment on the deck of the boat, just like he was stringing a needle, by trying to avoid getting the basket caught on the cranes and the fishing pots to evacuate the fisherman to the hospital to save his life. That's when it really dawns on me how scared and precious life is, and we should do everything that is humanly possible to preserve life.

I have come to realize how important technology is in the world today. It is a huge gold mine of information, entertainment, social media, and communication for everyone on this planet, especially for the disabled. I had no clue what I was missing when I was out there driving my cab. The only use I knew of for my phone was to make and receive phone calls and text messaging. I had boxes and boxes of compact disc in my cab for playing music. I had no clue what Wi-Fi was. I heard my customers talking about it, but I was too busy making money to care about what that was. I had no clue what Facebook or Twitter was. All my customers were going crazy about social media, but I couldn't care less at that time. The moment that I got disabled and was stuck in the house, I tried to listen to my favorite reggae radio station on my radio, and the reception was very bad with a lot of static, and I could not hear anything at all. I was so upset and disappointed, so my wife said to me, why don't you buy a pair of Bose computer speakers and plug them into the computer in the bedroom that you barely look at. So, I took her advice and bought the pair of speakers and plugged them into the computer, and I pulled up the tune in radio app, and I found my favorite reggae radio station. It was coming in crystal clear. That was the first time in my life that I had used the computer to stream music. The tune in radio app has over 100,000 radio stations from all over the globe. Every genre of music that you could imagine, every sport, talk radio, breaking news, comedy, and weather station is streaming on there in real time. I was like a kid in a candy store, suddenly this new world of technology opened to me. Although my mobility is limited, I could take full advantage of the opportunity that was available to me. I could learn about YouTube music and videos. I joined at least four different stroke support groups on Facebook, where I could connect with other stroke survivors like myself, who encourage me, lift me up, and understand my struggle. I can't put in words how grateful I am to my cable provider who help me and my family with affordable high-speed internet connection, Wi-Fi service, house phone, cable TV, and cellphone for a very small price per month. When I signed up with them as a new customer on May 7th, 2015, two weeks later, they sent me a debit card with a few hundred dollars that helped me with my rent because my Social Security Disability Benefits had not kicked in at the time. They also sent us movie tickets and other coupons. They don't know this, but me and my family will be forever grateful to them for always working with us many times with all the different payment arrangement they have allowed us when I do not have the full amount, many times.

Many disabled individuals, including veterans in our region and across America, do not realize what a huge resource this company can be to them and other low-income families who can benefit from this precious resource like I'm doing right now. I watched this company grow from a small company in the 1990's when they were called GSC to the power house that they are today in providing cutting edge technology that really help disabled individuals with devices, like the smart remote that you can talk into to find whatever channel you want to watch, show reminders, and have the ability to let you see when someone is at your front door without you having to get up from your seat. This is a part of their security package that they will install free of charge when you pay a few more dollars per month on your bill, and they also offer business internet. My family and I are customers for life, and that is why I am telling everyone that I know, especially disabled individuals or disabled veterans, who can run a business from home by utilizing this resource. Likewise, struggling families can be connected to lightning fast high-speed internet so that their children can study and do their homework at home.

I did massive amounts of research online, especially for writing this book in the privacy of my home. I learned so much information that I did not know existed. As a reggae and smooth jazz lover, I realized that I could go way back in time and watch different reggae and smooth jazz concerts that happened decades ago that I had missed in the past, and I could now watch concerts and stage shows in real time. I did not miss a beat, although I am disabled. I could go online and design my own unique style of t-shirts and sweatshirts for my own personal fund raiser and the good thing about that, I can always go back and start it up again whenever I'm ready to start fund raising again because it stays there permanently. There is Google that I used to get answers to any question that I needed to be answered.

Every man, woman, and child on this planet lives are touched by technology, whether directly or indirectly. I have come to rely on technology more than ever before since I lost the use of my left arm. I go to YouTube videos and watch how to do certain tasks, like how to install an EZ pass reader in my wife's car by using one hand, and it showed me how to unbox my computer printer, set it up, and install it without calling and bothering anyone for help. I used to ask for help with a lot of things, but YouTube video is my best friend. Now, I can always rely on it for help with most things and being entertained at the same time, which means I'm always having fun when I am working,

I just started to realize that a person can get more things done from home these days instead of getting in a car and spend a whole day going from place to place to take care of business and at the end of the day, you do not get a lot done. Just recently my favorite reggae disc jockey, 'Selecta Jerry," gave me a pair of tickets to go to the Annual Reggae in the Park stage show at the Mann Music Center in Philadelphia, and I gave both tickets to my wife and my sister-in-law to go and enjoy the show because I am afraid of large crowds. So, I stayed home and watched the entire stage show from start to finish in real time on YouTube video. I had a front row seat all to myself, watching this beautiful stage show. The music was awesome because the sound coming from my two BOSE speakers was amazing. I think I had a better time watching and listening to the show in my t-shirt and shorts in the privacy of my air-conditioned home more than a lot of people who must fight traffic to go back and forth from the show and endure 100-degree weather.

Technology is amazing, and it is getting better and better every day. I remember about three years ago we had Microsoft Windows 7 on our computer, and it crashed a lot and was constantly catching viruses, and I had to unplug it and take it to the computer repair shop for them to clean it, which could be a three-day process sometimes. Now we have Microsoft Windows 10, which is a much better program because it refreshes itself constantly. It is now more than three years, and the computer has not crashed one time.

I do not know what I would do without my computer. It compensates me by almost replacing my left hand, which I am unable to use. I buy everything online these days from my groceries to razor blades and everything in between. Before my wife bought her Jeep, she could take a virtual tour of the vehicle from the engine to the entire interior of the vehicle before she went into the dealership to see if she was going to buy the vehicle. I see people are beginning to live stream television channels from the Internet for as little as $7.00 to $20.00 per month, and sometimes it's free. They can also buy the Amazon fire stick to plug into their smart TV and if they have Wi-Fi service in their home, they can watch hundreds of channels from around the globe.

We did not have options like this even five years ago. With technology so plentiful these days, we now have unlimited options, and many more services are popping up online every day. I also become very familiar with the free video calling service by the name of WhatsApp where I can see the other person when we are talking on the phone. This service has been around for about four years, but I did not know anything about it until recently a friend of mine turned me on to it. If your cellphone service is suspended and you have Wi-FI, you can still use your phone to do everything that you need to do on the phone. You can see and talk to anyone anywhere in the world, and it is free. It also comes with free text messaging. A lot of people do not realize how much money they are losing by using data. There is portable Wi-Fi devices that can be fully charged, just like how you charge a cellphone, then you can take it with you anywhere, even when you go on vacation overseas, you will have reliable Wi-Fi service. These devices can be bought online, or they can be rented from your cell phone providers. I pay very little for my cellphone bill because I'm always on Wi-Fi. Back in the day, disabled people use to be the invisible population locked away from society and now technology has given us a voice and the ability to participate in today's world. We can now organize ourselves into whatever organizations or community groups and other types of civic engagements. Technology is moving so fast that we can't even keep up with it. My grandson is seven-years-old, and he can't even keep up with it. I am teaching him how to use WhatsApp because he has never heard of it, and he is teaching me how to use Tango because I have never heard of it as well, and now there is artificial intelligence of which I could write a whole book about.

My step-grandson and my best friend, T.J.

My local cable company has an entire division that is dedicated to hiring veterans and their families. They also provide internet service to under-served areas in every region that they service at very low and affordable rates. They give you free anti-virus protection of the finest quality so that your computers, phones, and all your devices run smoothly without catching viruses.

I used to spend lots of money buying anti-virus software that I had to renew every two years, which was a nightmare. With my local cable company, I have their anti-virus protection for life if I am a customer with them. I just have my son and his family to sign up with their internet service. The service will include wifi, and they will be using the cable company's cell phone service, which will include latest phones on the market today. All that costs less than $100.00 per month. They will be saving hundreds of dollars a year. Prior to that they were paying hundreds of dollars a year just for cell phone service.

Gishard — my son and his family with Donald

For years they were very limited to what they could do with their phones. However, with the new phone service, they have a variety of options. They don't have to be billed for using too much data or overages. My local cable company network was built to save consumers money. I highly recommended them to family and friends.

Many people are paying outrageous cable and phone bills in America because they do not know about this awesome opportunity to save thousands of dollars a year! I am so happy that I am with this company as my cable, Internet, and phone provider. I am fully wired, and without their services it would be very difficult to write my book. Whenever people realize how much money they are going to save by choosing them as their cable company provider, other companies will have to drop their prices for the consumer or risk going out of business.

Before I became a customer with them I used to have cell phone services with several cell phone companies. When I tried to listen to music or watch videos, after a few short hours, the data would slow down. When I would call customer service to see what was going on they would tell me I had gone over my data plan even though they would advertise unlimited data, which was not true of the plan.

Now that I have wifi built into my cable service I can go to bed with the music playing and wake up with the music playing without ever being over my data plan. I don't have to turn it off ever because the network refreshes and updates constantly. The network is very safe, especially for businesses. They are so far ahead of everyone else in the market. They are constantly upgrading and advancing in technology for consumers to set up their home wifi network service to find their password, see what devices are connected, troubleshoot issues, set parental control, and even pause wifi access on their home network. During dinner or bedtime it gives customers visibility and control over the most important technology in their homes at no extra cost.

## Doctor Gets Forty-five Years in Prison

It was reported on September 17, 2014 that a Detroit-area cancer doctor plead guilty to fraud, admitting he knew his patients did not need chemotherapy. The doctor plead guilty to sixteen charges including money laundering and conspiracy, without the benefit of a plea deal with prosecutors, who said they would not negotiate such a "shocking" and disturbing case. They would "seek a sentence of life in prison as [they] were not interested in bargaining anything away because his conduct was so egregious," said prosecutors on the courthouse steps. It was not a matter of stealing money but torturing patients by lying to them about having cancer. Chemotherapy is poison intended to kill cancer cells in the human body.

The doctor plead guilty one month before trial in Detroit Federal Court. The hearing was supposed to be an opportunity to argue about evidence, including an email that showed his interest in a three-million-dollar castle in his native country of Lebanon, at the peak of the scheme.

The US District Judge went over the charges and asked the doctor each time, "You are pleading guilty willingly and voluntarily?"

"Yes," he replied dressed in jail clothes.

His defense attorney did not explain the doctor's decision and later declined to comment when reached by phone. He told the judge that he and the doctor had met more than fifty times to discuss the evidence.

Patients and relatives of former patients were stunned when charges were filed. They protested the doctor on the courthouse sidewalk, and they keep in touch with each other for moral support. His cancer clinics had seven offices and a related business that performed tests to look for cancer. The government says the doctor submitted two hundred and twenty-five million dollars to Medicare over six years, about half for chemotherapy and other cancer treatments. Medicare paid more than ninety-one million dollars and private insurers were billed, too.

One relative of a patient said his father died in 2008, a year after being diagnosed with leukemia. He recalled the eighty-one year old getting treatment while sitting in the doctor's parking garage.

"The doctor told my dad it would make it easier. His kidneys eventually failed," the relative said.

When the doctor went in front of the judge for sentencing the judge called him "the most egregious fraudster in the history of the United States; to him patients were not people, they were profit centers."

The doctor gave an emotional apology in court, saying he was ashamed of his actions.

"I have violated the Hippocratic Oath and violated the trust of my patients." The doctor said, "I don't know how I can heal the wounds, I don't know how to express the sorrow and shame." But to hundred of his victims who filed into US District Court for the Eastern District of Michigan throughout the week to watch his sentencing, his apology does not matter. Many will live with the effects of his unnecessary treatments for the rest of their lives. The wife of one former patient said in court many were tortured until their last breath.

One of the patients went to the doctor and was given chemotherapy for two-and-a-half years. But he never had cancer. The chemotherapy treatments were so painful they made him physically sick. They were so strong his teeth fell out and his jaw started to change shape. Years after, he found out he did not have cancer, and he'd loss all but one of his teeth.

The doctor, according to his web page and flyers, was world-renowned. When you went into his office he was top doc. Before being sentenced the doctor turned toward those who were at his sentencing and again apologized: "The quest for power is self-destructive. They came to me seeking compassion and care. I failed, yes, I failed, yes, I failed."

The judge was not buying his apology and sentenced him to forty-five years in prison. The doctor is expected to serve at least thirty-four years of his sentence, possibly at a low-security prison in Michigan.

How on Earth could something like this happen in the United States of America? The system in this country enables this type of behavior. This doctor misdiagnosed over five-hundred-and-thirty patients for years, some of who died under his care. The judge gave him a slap on the wrist. This monster should have been given a life sentence without the possibility of parole.

The regulations and oversight of doctors and medical services in the US stinks to high heaven, and there is still a frontier medicine mindset that persists, which is rotten and disgusting like a dog that eats his own vomit. Where is the outrage in America? The American people should immediately demand that Congress abolish the statute of limitation on medical malpractice cases immediately.

When my ex-coworker stopped by to check on me recently as he always does from time to time, he was very surprised when I showed him things that he had never seen before. He still brings me compact discs with music on it that I do not need because I do not even have a cd player in my house. Any music that I could ever think of is in my phone, any style, any beat, and any rhythm. My ex-coworkers are still playing compact disc in their taxi cabs, and they are still listening to am/FM radio and not keeping up with modern technology,

They are still using their flip phones to make and receive calls and for texting. They are still stuck where I left them on March 10th, 2015 when I did my surgery. They are so busy working that they do not have the time to be curious about technology but because I am stuck in the house for the past two and a half years, I have all the time in the world to familiarize myself with technology and learn new things every day. I learned about bluetooth technology for the first time when I went with my wife to pay her bill at her favorite electronic store, and one of the sale associate demonstrated to me how bluetooth speakers worked with my cellphone. I fell in love with it immediately, and I bought me a bluetooth portable speaker sound system that I can take with me whenever I go out of state or when I'm away from home, so I can listen to my favorite radio stations or watch movies from my phone that I often download from Netflix or from my cable provider, which I find to be very convenient. The Internet is so vast and expansive. It's like another planet onto itself, and we are living on it. There is no person alive today who can fully utilize every platform on the Internet, that is totally impossible to do. I am on the computer now for the past two and a half years, and I do not even scratch the surface of knowing much of the things that I need to know. The way that I see it is that you must pick your spots and work with just a few platforms on the internet. That is very good because people can use the platforms that they like. The exception that really stands out to me is Facebook. It is unique, everybody loves it. Young and old people. The good thing about it is if you are searching for a long-lost friend or relative, chances are you can find them on Facebook, and sometimes people are searching for you as well.

I think that it is safe to say that almost everyone has a Facebook page. This is a very interesting time to be alive. I have seen on the news that a certain ride share company is introducing driverless cars that you can order from your computer or from your phone. I believe that once the technology is perfected, that will be a huge win for disabled individuals, which would give them respect and independence. I can't believe that I live to see the world change before my eyes because of innovation in technology, and I am benefiting from it.

I grew up very poor, and I remember the days when it took three days for my mother to receive a telegram from my brother when he was working in Guantanamo Bay. We had no radio and no television. My friends and I had to walk for miles to go and watch television at a lady's house, mostly on Saturday's after finishing my chores. We used to sit on her porch and watch Bonanza and Voyage to the Bottom of the Sea. We were not allowed in her living room because she was afraid of us soiling her furniture.

This is now the future, and I am embracing it because it is getting better and better every day. When I bought my first flip-phone, I thought it was the best thing since sliced bread. I had no clue that they could have made phones any better than that. The smart phone that I have now is basically a mini computer that can hold all the information from the library of congress, and my phone carrier is calling me every day to come and upgrade my phone. It's like I cannot keep up. My phone can be submerged in water for hours and still work after taking a beating. You can do everything from your phone these days, like see who is at your front door even if you are on vacation or if someone is trying to commit a crime on your property or laying in wait to ambush you. When someone rings your door bell, it rings on your phone, and you will see who it is right away anywhere in the world you are. You can use the phone to turn the lights on and off in your house or to start your car. They come standard with flash lights on them and when bad weather is on the way, you always get an alert on your phone warning you to take cover. On June 23rd, 2015, a tornado was on the ground in my township, and everyone in my household got a warning on their phone to take cover immediately. That was the first time that I knew cell phones had that capability. It helps law enforcement to solve crimes quickly or help someone who is in distress; for example, if someone goes missing on a hiking trip and their phone dies, it allows rescuers to pinpoint the last location where your phone pinged. This has led to many people being found alive. It is also a useful tool to find people who have been kidnapped.

A few years ago, I was listening to a local FM radio station that broadcasts from a nearby county college and a few hours into the broadcast, a freak storm passed through and blew down their transmitters, and the station went off the air, and I used my cellphone to access their website and continued to listen to the program. It shows that the benefit of technology is endless when it comes to communication, transportation, medicine, security, construction, energy, and education.

I must admit that the downside to technology is that it is much easier for criminals or people with bad intentions to do harm to people who are vulnerable. We let people in our homes these days through our devices who we would not allow to come to our front door in any way, shape, or form, and that is why the authorities are always reminding people not to give out their physical address, phone number, or e-mail address on the Internet. People need to use common sense when surfing online because a tech savvy person can find your location quickly from any information that you volunteered. It is a good idea to turn off the locator on your phone because there are a lot of dangerous people out there. The good thing is that the good outweighs the bad when it comes to technology. Another danger that is lurking on the internet is some of those dating websites because more and more people are going online looking for love, and there is so much deception where people are setting up fake profiles to lure people who are looking for a certain type of woman or man and most of the time, those photos are Photoshopped to make it look real.

A few years ago, I was watching a program on the Discovery channel name *Web of Lies* and saw where this 38-year-old man set up a fake profile pretending that he was a 16-year-old teenager. And he lured this 16-year-old girl from her house in the middle of the night, raped her, killed her, and put her body in a 45-gallon drum and buried it in the ground. Because of some great detective work he was caught, tried, and was sentenced to life in prison. Another story that really breaks my heart that I saw on the same network is a single mom who was very lonely and went online looking for love and met a gentleman that she really liked from his profile. They had arranged to go on a date, and she left her kids home, and she told them she would be back. She did not return home because she thought the person she was going to meet was this handsome man she met online, but it was a fake profile that her ex-husband created by Photoshopping it online, and he lured her from her home and murdered her. The investigation into this case was very frustrating and time consuming for the detectives and law enforcement. When the investigators went back and checked her computer, the Facebook profile disappeared without a trace. The only way that they found out that her ex-husband was the culprit, they saw in her cellphone he was the last person that she had texted right before she disappeared. He lied to the investigators initially that he had not seen or heard from her in years, so they subpoena his phone records, and that is how they caught him and was able to charge him with first degree murder. He was convicted in Federal Court and was sentenced to life in prison.

The reason why I shared a few of these stories that I've watched on *Web of Lies* is to let people be aware of how cunning and ruthless people with bad intentions can be. The disable population, especially, is very vulnerable because they sometimes are very trusting of strangers. Not purposely but sometimes out of necessity. I remember I had a customer when I was driving my taxi, and she had a stroke and was paralyzed just like I am now. She would call me many times and pay me to bring in her motorized scooter in her house for her, or sometimes she would give me her ATM card to go to the bank to make withdrawals for her. My wife and I did a lot of things to help her because she lived alone. When she had the stroke, her kids abandoned her and said that she was too much of a burden on them. She told me that she fell on the floor and laid there for three days until her landlord came and found her when he came to collect the rent. She was very trusting of whoever came around her. She was always asking someone to do things for her, and she paid them. She had a very independent spirit, but she was not physically able to do very much for herself. I suggested to her to get life alert, which is a device that can be worn around your neck and if you fall and can't get up, you can squeeze the emergency button on it, and they will have someone respond immediately to provide assistance. She took my advice and got one, and she told me that she finally would have some peace of mind because she wanted to live in the privacy of her own home, without having to go to an assisted living residence where the treatment can be very bad.

I do hope that I recover from this nightmare soon. When I wake up every morning and look outside and see the empty parking spaces and realize that all my neighbors are gone to work, it drives me crazy, and sometimes I feel like a loser. This should never have happened to me, but I give God thanks every day that I am still alive. Although I still have the blood clot lodged deep in my brain, I am blessed that I am mostly in my right mind to be able to write this book. I must check every word that I write at least five times to make sure it is what I really want to say. Anyone who has ever experienced brain damage knows how difficult it is to remember anything, much less write a book.

I must admit that I am very disgusted and disappointed every time I remember how much I have lost, and I know that I might never recover my losses. I know for sure that I will lose my commercial driver's license (CDL) because everyone that has one of these licenses must take a physical every two years to keep it updated. Despite all of this that happened to me, I am thankful to God for saving my life.

A series of beautiful picture from my fellow stroke survivors group to cheer me up.

My Motto